Y 189   443

Runes
Letters to my son

DATE	ISSUED TO
4/11	Emil P's

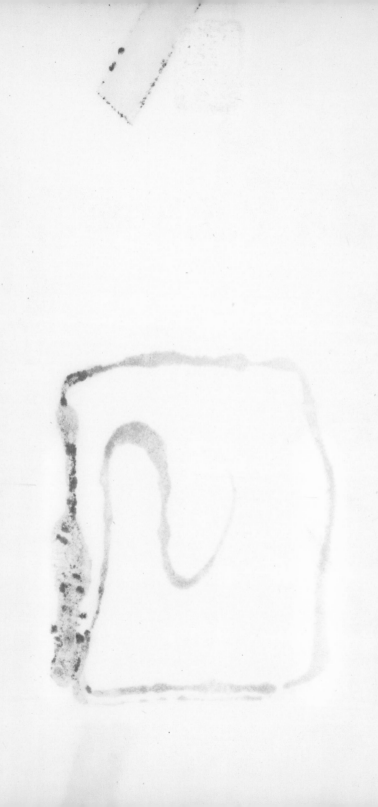

Letters
TO MY SON

Letters
to My Son

BY

DAGOBERT D. RUNES

PHILOSOPHICAL LIBRARY

New York

443

To my Mother,

VICTIM OF TEUTONIC FURY

Table of Contents

Letters
TO MY SON

.

The People of the Book

MY DEAR SON,

A wise man once said that if a truly good thing perishes, a hole remains in the world. How many things do you possess that would leave a hole in the world, were they to disappear? Look about you, look inside yourself, and look behind you. There are those close to you, those who raised you on the palms of their hearts, those who befriended you in your searchings and in your play. And then there is the vastness of things behind you, ahead of you, and around you. We live in an ocean of things, but few are of beauty and few are of merit. There would be no hole in the world were they to disappear—the things that man created to lead a more comfortable life.

It would matter little if man were never again to raise a plane into the sky, if he were never to yoke the power of steam and never to bind the lightning of electricity and the thunder of the atom into his relentless harness. All these toys of man's dabbling in creation are but motes of dust on the million surfaces of the universe, and their clatter and noise in man's haste for better comfort is drowned out by the interior music of the spheres.

Walk into the meadow on a moonlit night and look upon the trillion stars, gaze upon the trillion planets that are riding with you the course of infinite eternity. Perhaps your eyes will feel the distant music of the Gods.

There is little to what man creates, unless it is in the service of creation. And what man manufactures and what man mentor-factures—these things will not leave a hole in the world even if they were all to go out and vanish in one blast.

Yes, there is one thing, one single thing that will endure—that is the Book.

Legend has it that the first book was the Torah, the only testament that God handed down to man. And to distinguish the people to whom he gave the Book from the rest of the world, he called them *Am-ha-safer*—the people of the Book.

The Hebrew religion refuses to crown its priests, unlike the other churches of the Western world, which adorn their priests and ministers with crowns and rings and purple cloth. The Hebrews place their crown upon the Torah. It matters not how tiny the synagogue, its Torah carries a crown. No rabbi may bedeck his flesh and bone with the crowning vestment. The Hebrews are *Am-ha-safer* —the people of the Book—and the Book is king.

So goes the legend of the Torah. But the people of the Book are few, very few. And the Book is still the only chain between man and the Eternal.

Somewhere in the Himalayas there may be a man who is closer to you than the million people in your city. Man's closeness to God may be measured by his proximity to the Book, and that man in the Himalayas may stand on the very steps you do, before the same page and the same line of the same Book.

You may be bound to him by the same faith, the religion of the Book. Indeed, the word religion means *binding*.

The world brings forth a million books—sheets

of paper, printed, folded, and bound like things of greatness. But they are nothing more than toys in the rush for comfort and amusement.

Books written by harlots too old to sin but not too feeble to write;

books by hacks who write for a living with journalistic ease and felicity;

books by aging generals and statesmen who find it profitable to describe their diplomatic double-deeds and carnages of war to an amusement-hungry public;

books by teachers who for the sake of a career set down on paper unwanted and never-read dissertations on abstruse subjects, meant to prove the learning of the author;

books of contrived poetry by bearded loafers with an adolescent appearance, who by being different cash in on a never-dying mode;

books by big-shots, from president to storekeeper, where a ghost is the real author and the author a mere ghost.

There are confidence men in literature as well as in finance, business and politics. We have Huey Longs and Staviskys in all the fine arts. There always will be Ezra Pounds in literature, people who by sheer publicity stunts make themselves conspicuous, so that all they need is some clever —if meaningless—literary stunt to plant themselves on top of the heap. Although they leave nothing for the future and give nothing to the present, they usurp the attention, acclaim and monetary rewards that are due the truly creative.

YOUR LOVING

FATHER

On Friendship

My dear Son,

You still remember the story of the shepherd who cried "Wolf," though he saw only some shadow moving across the hill or heard some bird scraping the brush or a twig falling from a tree. When the wolf really came, no one heeded the shepherd's cries.

Few are the words in our language that have a meaningful depth of their own, and those you ought not to use in vain. One of these words is *friend*.

How casually that word is tossed about. Frequently it is used to mean something that is its exact opposite. Often a friend is a person known well enough to be envied for his successes and enjoyed for his troubles.

Too often are such close relationships founded on dislike and envy, called friendships, for we are bound to those we hate almost as much as to those we love. Perhaps hatred is even a stronger tie than affection; it is more lasting, and like love, seeks out its object, yearning to dwell in its shadow.

A true friend, my son! There lies some of life's everlasting essence.

A thousand books and papers have been written, a thousand sermons delivered, on the wonders of friendship. Like all wonderful things, it is rare and difficult to explain. Like all things rooted in affection, friendship strikes one suddenly; but one can't let it go at that. Friends must be cultivated patiently and persistently once that initial spark is ignited.

Your friend is the one who sees you as you would love to see yourself. To your friend you are the image of your own dreams and hopes.

You may be a skinny, pimply-faced, squeaky-voiced youth—if your thoughts are heroic, to your friend you are Siegfried smiting the dragon, you are Achilles avenging the rape of Helen.

You may be a squat, moon-faced little grocer, eagerly dabbling in over-the-counter politics—to your friend you seem erect and wise, pregnant with statesmanship.

You may be a red-faced, flat-footed hulking cop —to your friend you are in your shining new uniform a Big man, the upholder of law and order.

You may be a poorly-nourished, nervous pedantic schoolmaster—to your friend you are a courageous bearer of the torch of learning and civilization.

You may be a dirty, filthy, moneybag, desirous only of multiplying itself quicker than a pair of mice—to your friend you are a great visionary entrepreneur.

You may be a common thief, a second-story man or mugger, a pickpocket or racketeer—to your friend you are a smart guy who is wised up to this sucker world.

Your friend will always see you as you imagine yourself in your dreams. Perhaps that is what makes him your friend; he can see you as you want to be, as you could be, not as you really are.

The mere sight of your friend must elevate you. You feel better now, you feel inspired and happy. Your friend has entered the room.

Do you still recall that you once asked me how a crab can love a crab? Well, he can. There is no one ugly, despicable, malformed, mal-thinking and mal-doing enough not to find a friend. There is a lover even for a crab. Thersites, the ugliest of the Greeks, even he had a friend.

Like the Stone of Wisdom, friendship may be lying right in your back yard and you may never know it. Your best friend may be a stranger to you, or you may lose him because you didn't bother to hold him.

Friends must be cultivated by sincerity, frankness, and deeds of affection. No one can remain your friend if you hide your soul from him.

You needn't save face before your friend. Your friend will save it for you.

Life is a chain of little events. Close your soul to your friend and he will lose sight of you. And if you find your friend, give of your friendship and it will return to you tenfold. Those who cannot give friendship will rarely receive it and never hold it.

YOUR LOVING
FATHER

You Are Only a Guest

MY LITTLE MAN,

As you know, I have never addressed you as "my little child" the way people are accustomed to address children. They like to create two worlds, the world of the child and the world of man. In the world of the child virtue seems to abound, justice to flower, and kindness and tolerance to flourish. Ah, but in the world of man the ways are crooked, the designs evil, and the interests malicious. And so they let you live your early years in the childhood world of make believe only to awaken you when maturity takes you into the reality of a most sorrowful existence. And while you still rub your eyes—were you dreaming? were you seeing things?—all the pretty, warm and playful children grow into mean, designing, envious men and women.

It was all right for you, my little man, to play with a colored girl with marbles and hoop and swing; but now if you were only to walk down the street with her hand-in-hand, they would point their fingers at you and cast you from their group like a leper.

It was all right for you, my son, to share your cot with the German lad; but now the school which he enters is closed to you and you must hunt for your learning until you find a back bench that they have put aside for you perhaps a thousand miles away.

That is why I never called you "child," my little man. I didn't want you to rise too high in the skyward climb of early dreams, only to fall on the rocky face of this infested globe.

Remember when I took you to that little town in Georgia and seated you in a classroom and you listened to a wise old teacher talk about American democracy and freedom for all and the pursuit of happiness, and how I suddenly poked you in the ribs and you began to cry and asked me why? I told you, "Don't be a dreamy fool. Just wait." And I took you across the street into the park and showed you the public fountain. Upon the stony base was engraved, "For whites only." And I told you of another park in another country where the schools were even better and bigger than in

Georgia and the churches more cathedral. There was a beautiful sandy beach, but in the center a huge placard said, "Jews Keep Out."

That fountain-base in Georgia, that placard in Germany, were not put up by evil-minded persons who live on the fringe of the community. These ugly deeds were perpetrated by the people in authority, by the very same people who teach their children democracy and preach the good Christian life to them in their churches.

They have made a mint of words, these people, but these words are not coins any longer. They are chips. There is neither gold in them nor silver, only some worthless plastic which they pass to each other in secret and open gentlemen's agreements—and just try to cash these chips. Let a Negro man try to ask for full value at work or at play or even at prayer. The very man who preaches that all men are God's children, equal before Him and the Holy Ghost and the loving Christ, would turn him out of church.

If you are a Hebrew there are a thousand schools that will not accept you, a thousand homes that will not house you, a thousand bosses who will not hire you.

Democracy, equality, dignity—these are chips, my son, not coins. They may be cashed only by members, and never forget that although you and your black brother may often be guests, you can never be members. It is odd that some of these chips should bear the likeness of Christ—*Love Thy Neighbor* is the engraved motto. Others bear the motto of Moses; the *Ten Commandments* are on their reverse side. Both were Israelites; one even an African born on the Nile. Perhaps these coins were cut only in irony—how little do these people love their Israelite neighbors, and have the Commandments ever been applied to the Africans?

Since you were knee-high, my son, I have taught you the worthlessness of these coins. Six millions of your brothers and sisters were poisoned and burned, hunted, tortured, drowned and bludgeoned, butchered and choked, garroted and guillotined, denounced and strung up by seventy million well-educated Christians living in the heart of Europe. And the world of Christian men went about its business, deaf to the cries of mothers who saw their children cut up before their eyes, of children who were made to watch the agonies of their choking parents. You see, even then, in the face of these most devilish of abominations, the people of the Christian world were not concerned with the fate of your victimized brothers and sisters. They would rather forgive the skinning alive of your brothers than forget your own slightest transgression.

There are no children among the beleaguered, my son. We Israelites live on a rock surrounded by an ocean of hate, suspicion, and indifference, and we never know when and where the next storm may come. You must be alert, my son, alert and fighting-ready. You can never really be a child in such turmoil. Never fear so long as you stand on the rock of Israel's heritage and so long as you do not let them set you to dreaming with their sirenic fables and promises. You have only one friend, my son, and that is your courage. And like that mythological figure of old, when you leave the rock of your heritage, gone is your strength and your future. Be strong, my son.

YOUR LOVING

FATHER

God Looks at You

MY DEAR SON,

You asked me the other day what people look like to God. I really do not know. But as the Great Being wanders among the planets, the people on this globe must look tiny to Him. A bit of difference in color here, a slight variation in size there, but from afar they must all look alike. Can you tell one bee from another or one ant from another? Yet no two are the same.

Of course, little people make much of the little which makes them different from another, but to the aeons eternalizing the universe, man differs from man as barely as a dust grain varies from a dust grain.

Remember when we looked down from the top of the hill and watched the brown horses, the grey, the white, and the black. From afar, they all seemed pretty much alike.

Yet so many people seem to get a kick out of blowing up their tiny differences into fundamentals. If they would only take the trouble to walk to the top of the hill, how small and how much alike appear all creatures, deep down below in the valley of speeding time and dwindling space.

The black of the dark-skinned races, the yellow of the Eskimo, the brown of the Malayan, and the obscureness of the European—all these little colors become one in the great glaring light of the universe.

How little we know of our races, if after a million years we are aware of only a few thousand! Suppose a man could trace his ancestors back to the time of Plato, how infinitesimally short a time he has covered. Suppose even that he could go back still another step, and trace another interval of the same length. The rest is darkness, as far as man is concerned, and eternity. He can scarcely glimpse a thread in the hem of ancient man, and yet he speaks of races, attempting to divide mankind on the basis of what he has learned from two little steps backward in time. What folly, and what conceit!

God cannot see the marks and markings by which humans distinguish themselves from each other. He can but see the humans.

Nevertheless, humans differ even before God. *Not* in pigmentation nor hirsuteness, not in shrewdness nor skill, but in their souls they differ.

A thousand things distinguish man before man, but only one distinguishes man before God—his conscience. Nothing else matters, nothing else carries weight inside this worldly tumult.

If you scratch the surface, the good are not so good; neither are the bad so evil. There are but two kinds of humans—the conscientious and the unprincipled.

The man who stops his car as he drives by a wounded creature and the man who would run—even had he hit one—these two personify the only real good and evil in personal character. The hiker who drops a burning match as he leaves a forest; the selfish friend who denies assistance to his fallen comrade; the son who turns from his needy mother, the convert who deserts his suffering tribe; the schemer who intrigues from opportunity to opportunity; the neighbor who doesn't harken to the call for help; the stony self-seeker who turns his back when the weak are molested; the peace-hog who scuttles for his ivory tower when the enemy sets out upon his sinister raids—these are the men without conscience.

A million starry miles from the earth, the ugliness of those petrified hearts can be felt.

Does it matter in which church they pray if their prayers are but the greedy dreams of their selfish desires? Glory be to those blessed who pray that they may give and help.

Pleasure, in itself, is not virtue; neither is misery. But bringing pleasure to others is virtuous and bringing misery is immoral.

Such is the light of conscience that without it

man stumbles in the darkness of his ego, crawling from greed to fulfillment and from fulfillment to desire, but the inner light of self-satisfaction will never be kindled in him.

Nevertheless, the pleasure of giving, the pleasure of helping, the pleasure of defending is greater than all the trappings of avarice. The love that is spent on others will come back a thousandfold.

There are only two kinds of men: those with love and conscience before God and man, and those who are hardened into the rocky nothingness of self-centered indifference.

In His far-away wisdom the Lord cannot but see this great divide, the Lord Eternal before Whose sun of awareness the foolish body distinctions between man and man disappear like the vapor they are.

YOUR LOVING
FATHER

Courage of the Mind

My dear Son,

To speak of courage is to speak of two things: the courage of the body and the courage of the mind.

Courage of the body you can see in the fury of the tiger, the madness of the bull, the cold viciousness of the snake. They care not for what dangers lie in the path of their attack. Their muscles are tense; tendons strained and eyes glowing, they're set to kill. Perhaps theirs is some premonition of danger, some dumb feeling of possible disaster; but in that tantrum born of hunger or vengeance or fear, there is no room for second thought—or any thought. Theirs is the courage of the man amuck—the courage of the body.

Also there is courage in the gambling man; the daredevil who jumps over the waterfall in a barrel; the woman who flies the trapeze a hundred feet above the hard arena, nothing between her and a horrible death but the delicate sense of human balance; the reckless show-off, the man who runs his car down a ravine or takes a dare to float his canoe through whirling currents. There, too, is no room for second thought. The mania for a chance accomplishment blinds these men to odds, the hundred-to-one gamble. The greed of the body's affectations is greater here than the dictates of reason or human values. They stake their lives on a dare, their fortunes on the turn of a roulette wheel, minds beclouded by the hashish of the hazard. This also is the courage of the body.

There is yet another courage—born neither of fear nor fury nor reckless forgetfulness—the courage conceived in the mind.

The furious and the gamblers—they shut their eyes to the mind and jump. But the truly courageous look danger in the eye and walk the path where humans fear to tread.

Fearlessness is shown not so much by those who stoically accept an inevitable verdict of death, but rather by those who could escape the death penalty if they would only submit.

The Rabbis of old, who walked the burning

planks of the Roman conquerors rather than desert their faith and their faithful; Socrates, the teacher who preferred taking hemlock poison to keeping silent; Giordano Bruno, who perished rather than deny the living truth; Galileo, exclaiming before his theological executioners *"Eppur si muove,"* in order to serve science; the French revolutionaries, who fell on the barricades that the flag of freedom might stand aloft; the American Minutemen, who exposed their chests to the bullet lest freedom be deserted—these were men with *courage of the mind.*

Neither fury nor fear nor ferocity made them take their lives into their hands and toss them into carnage and turmoil. They wanted to live, and peacefully; they hated danger and scorned adventure. But more than they wished to live, they desired freedom. And they gave their lives that freedom might prevail.

Such acts of self-sacrifice might be called a form of suicide, and you will sometimes hear it said that suicide is the result of a kind of insanity. But in many instances suicide is the only sane escape from the insanity of a particular way of living. The great heroes who died by their own will sacrificed themselves that ideas might live— ideas which they treasured more highly than life.

All through history you will find these men and women, and were it not for them this would be a sorrier world than it is already, a world without hope. Whatever hope is ours today rests on the stoutness of the hearts of those whose courage is of the mind—not of the body.

YOUR LOVING

FATHER

The Failure of Success

There is no greater failure in life than success. The man who sets success as his goal is doomed to failure, since one desire for achievement succeeds another in the endless chain of human vanity.

There is no fulfillment in success; there is only elimination of one's competitor. It is all a matter of comparison. If men were to hold no jobs, there would be no drive to supersede them. If men were not to own yachts, there would be no wish to outsail them. If men were not to own the glitter and the false glory that monied power brings, there would be no desire to outshine them.

Success succeeds only in increasing desire—until all competition is eliminated. And until that time, along with the climbing go the burden, the strain, the envy, the fear, the false hope that always beckons before the climber, and the meanness and hardness that this type of competitive living entails.

The struggler for success has his eye glued on his competitor. Nothing matters beyond the need to outrun his opponents.

The success-minded man is surrounded by opponents and opposition in a self-created world of competitive dissatisfaction.

Glance along that road to success. You can see them stumbling on: the greasy moneybags, tinselly show-offs, phoney virtuosos, double-dealing politicians, and prostituted performers.

The road to success is crimson with crime and corruption.

Let me repeat, honor and wealth can be measured only by comparison. Among some people the greatest honor may be bestowed upon him who can dive deepest into the sea, or milk a cow faster than the next fellow. In some Hungarian villages, a boy going courting would rub his head against a horse's flank to smell horsey; only few of the farmers own horses and it shows caste to smell from them.

There is no honor or form of wealth the world

can bestow upon men that would not appear silly and meaningless in another part of the world, or in another age. The measure of true intelligence is the speed with which a man realizes the vanity of human honors and human wealth. The true values of living are sealed within man's own inner realm, but it takes depth and courage to attain them, and with them that majestic indifference towards the cheap trinkets that signify social honors and social wealth.

Neither can honor be offered by others. Honor must lie in one's self. Outsiders can judge only surface actions. The Self alone knows its true motives. The greatest deeds in history, as on the battlefield, remain unhonored by men; there was no witness, only the cosmic eye and man's own conscience.

True honor does not crave recognition, as true wisdom craves not publicity. The great heroes and the great men of wisdom walk silently through the bypaths of mankind.

From the sermons of the Preacher, to the meditations of Marcus Aurelius, that other kingly philosopher, to the psycho-mathematics of Baruch Spinoza, this thought seems closest to the Stone of Wisdom.

Remember, the true measure of success in life lies in production for use and the welfare of the community. And of all failings, the ugliest is the lust for personal success. Let you, my son, step aside and let humanity succeed.

YOUR LOVING
FATHER

Of the Laziness of the Heart

My dear Son,

You asked me what is right and what is wrong; what should you do, what should you avoid?

Well, there is no law worth obeying aside from the Law of the Heart.

People who obeyed the laws of politics, the laws of religion or the laws of custom have committed some of the most horrible crimes in history. The Nazi government in Germany, for instance, established a law calling for the extermination of what they called inferior races, and 70 million Germans plunged into a frenzy of legalized murder, the like of which the world hasn't seen since the days of the caveman.

Some Christian churches interpreted a symbolic admonition of Jesus Christ as a law to burn heretics, and for almost 2,000 years hundreds of millions of believers and their appointed religious representatives ran amuck in their *auto de fe*.

More people were burned alive by those blindly obeying this sacro-tragic law than were living in Palestine at the time Christ walked the streets of Jerusalem.

Do not think that these burnings took place thousands of years ago when people were supposed to be superstitious and ignorant. These legalized religious murders were still occurring at the time Benjamin Franklin kept shop in Philadelphia, at a time when men had the privilege of listening to liberal, far-sighted and good-hearted men. But evil laws got the best of the people. What bitterness will fill your heart when you read how in the century of Benjamin Franklin's birth, in good old England and in good old New England, fine and upright citizens were tied to a stake and burned alive over a slow and tiny fire. How many of them had their legs burned to a crisp while they shrieked, "Merciful God, why don't we burn faster?" And hundreds of citizens stood unmoved, nothing in their hearts but the icy righteousness of an evil religious law, watching the torturous sufferings of their neighbors.

So you see, my son, why I beg of you, do not obey "the law" but rather the Law of your Heart.

There are laws of custom, too, and one of these is the law practised in some of our states, where, if a man with a darker skin pigment than ours engages in a bodily encounter with that yellow type of man whom we choose to call white, the colored man is denied the protection of the laws and instead becomes the victim of a mob law of extermination. And men who otherwise seem to behave in a civilized manner become unbridled savages and executors of the law of Judge Lynch, thinking nothing of stringing up a colored boy, pouring kerosene over his twisting body, and giving him the torch. And again hundreds of men and women and children gather to watch this law of custom being carried out in their midst.

Do not obey any law, my son, neither the law of politics nor the law of religion nor the law of custom. Don't let the law be master of your heart. Let the heart master your conduct.

And do not let your heart be silent or acquiescing or forgetful. The world is full of evil laws and full of evil deeds executed and committed not only by those we know to be the bad and mean and cussedly wicked, but co-executed and co-committed by those millions upon millions who suffer from man's most loathsome disease, *the laziness of the heart.*

Don't let your heart become lazy, my son. He who condones a bad law or a bad deed is a perpetrator of dark evils, as guilty as the black ram that lures the other sheep to slaughter. Do not let your heart become lazy, but fight to break those terrible laws which chain the masses to that bitter treadmill in which they crush brethren. Let your heart speak, and do not stand in heart-hardened indifference when ignorance or corruption bewitches the people into seeing an outrage as a legalized custom of civilization.

Look about you, my son, and call out the true face of the things you see.

Don't let your heart become lazy and your voice sink to a whisper. He who neglects to fight the wrong is as guilty as he who commits it.

From the Book of Wisdom comes this simple guide, "Where there are stronger, stand on the side of the weaker."

Stand on the side of the weaker and you'll always be on the right side.

YOUR LOVING

FATHER

The Art of Silence

My dear Son,

A Rabbi said, "Chew your words before you send them from your mouth; if you do, you will find many you will wish to keep back and others that you will want to send forth with tender companions."

Did you ever watch people argue? They pick up a word thrown at them and hurl it back at the speaker in a barbed reply, giving the other fellow's words the worst possible meaning and their own the best.

So encrusted with words has our language become that people can argue for hours without discovering that each is using the words of the other, but with a different meaning in mind. The answers given, the arguments refuted, and even the questions raised in this rapid interchange of words, are all dictated by the overlapping patterns of prejudice, tradition, shifting opinion and thinking by rote.

If men would only rest in silence! Silence can be a most powerful argument. The beginning of our thinking is silence. The more thoughtless a person is, the less silence he requires. If they would only sit on their tongues instead of their ears—and keep silent. Silence is the first—and the most important—step to independent thought.

Only those who learn to keep silent can truly think through an idea. Silence is the beginning of philosophy. And perhaps also the end. Because where thought is at its deepest, silence reigns.

Man's deepest devotions and loftiest meditations have always drawn about them the mystic robe of silence.

Perhaps the greatest minds of all time, the greatest poets and artists, will never be known. They may be just such men of silence who have tossed away the word, the brush, and the lyre as the halting crutches of human frailty.

The greatest philosopher may never be known —like the demon of Socrates that never let him write, like the artists of old Israel from whom Jehovah had taken brush and chisel.

Perhaps the most ethereal poetry glows in the

soul of the man who stands on some lonely cliff gazing silently into the far sea at sundown; perhaps the greatest wisdom rests in the mind of some Carpathian shepherd who lives with the forest and the meadows in silent contemplation and has found the peace of God; perhaps the most overpowering music is in the ears of some village organist who, in his silent way, is closer to the songs of Heaven than the bushy-haired, frock-coated and white-gloved symphonic composer of our metropolis.

Perhaps the greatest works in philosophy and the arts have never been recorded because where creation is most intense, silence is deepest.

YOUR LOVING
FATHER

The People of the Ivory Tower

MY DEAR SON,

Idealism is an approach to life, not an end in itself. One can be quite materialistic about so-called ideal things, such as religion, literature and the arts. On the other hand, one can be quite idealistic about material things such as the living conditions of the working or farming man.

We have had great connoisseurs in history who filled their galleries with paintings, were the patrons of poets and preachers, and kept their farm folk in serfdom or beggary. Nevertheless they considered themselves idealists. We have fancy-pants today who flutter through museums and lecture halls with idealistic prattle, while half of God's living children may live or die for want of the simple material things that hold together body and soul.

I suspect the enemies of materialism. They either live off idealism or drape it about them-

selves like a cloak to keep from being touched by
the tears and sweat of the victims of materialism.

YOUR LOVING
FATHER

I Want You to Intervene

MY DEAR SON,

Do you remember the hot summer day when you and I sat by the bank of the brook? The leafy edge of the brook swarmed with insects—above the water, on the surface, and below. Some of them were so tiny you could hardly see them. There must have been a million more teeming there, so small that you could not find them even with a magnifying glass; a world with a million creatures in that little corner at the edge of the brook.

You asked me about all those insects and bugs, about the frogs and fish, the birds and the flies. Why were they all humming and swimming and flying about? What were they thinking of?

They all had but one thought in mind—to kill and devour, or to escape from being devoured.

The bank of that brook is just one of the unnumbered battlefields of nature. Only the battle never ends.

Who can fathom why nature is so designed that creatures can exist only by destroying other creatures?

The spider lives on the mosquito, the frog lives on the spider, and the stork on the frog. The bird lives on the worm and the hawk on the little bird. Wherever you turn, animals grow fat and greasy on the blood of other creatures. And where there are some blessed herds that eat grass instead of the insides of other animals, they are just being fattened for the flesh eaters.

This is the uncanny plan underlying existence on our globe. And man is no exception in this chain of butchery which begins at the edge of the brook and ends nowhere. The life's juice of the bug that was eaten by the worm which was eaten by the fish that you and I had for dinner is in your stomach and mine.

If this is the planning of nature, where can we find a guide for just living? Certainly not by imitating such devious planning.

We must place the scale of justice on a different

plane—a plane of our own creation, for the creatures of nature are monstrous.

It has been said that justice is like a pole claimed by two men. One man holds most of it and says it is his; another holds a tiny part of it and claims it for himself. Nevertheless, there *is* justice, although our life is so blackened and clouded by tradition, prejudice, greed, and animal hate, that only great strength of conscience and character can uncover it.

Few are the people who live by conscience. Too many of them live like the bug at the brook, killing the weaker and crawling away from the stronger. Perhaps it is easier to live without a conscience, and watch silently as the world goes by your door, chaining the weaker and bleeding the defenseless. Perhaps it is easier. But is this living?

I want you to live, my son, in pursuit of justice and not power. I want you to intervene on the side of the weaker and not let those who are stronger succeed in their sinful tasks.

I want you to intervene!

YOUR LOVING

FATHER

The Blessings of a Lie

My dear Son,

The most beautiful thing in the world, my son, is a "white" lie. How unbearable would our existence be were you to take away the flowers of deceit and make-believe and leave us the barrenness of mere truth.

A girl walks along the street, a girl with a thin face and pimples crowding each other; her heart is cold and her spirits low. She is an ugly duckling in all truth. A boy walks by enchanted by some mysterious urge of self-deception; he stops the girl and says, "How pretty you are, how pretty you are."

Perhaps this is not a deliberate lie; it certainly isn't the truth. But what can all the mighty powers of truth, what can they all mean against the soft breeze of that little lie: "How pretty you are."

A boy is lying in a field, a bullet in his spine. A chaplain whispers to a feverish mind, "You will

live, my son, live again in the arms of your mother,
live back in your home town with your baby sister
and your games and your boyhood friends."

The very promise of life grows from this
fatherly lie! How ugly would be truth were it to
befall this dying soldier.

I see an old woman laboring over a mountain of
other people's wash, her dress gingham, her hair
in strings, her furrowed forehead damp with per-
spiration and white her bluish hands.

For thirty years she labored for two, a worthless
son and her resigned self. Her gnarled fingers sent
him to school. His school years are over and he is
gone. For five years not a word, not a line to the
sad parent.

Her son is in a big city a thousand miles away.
He has grown rich on evil deeds. Someone recog-
nizes him. Shall he bring to the mother the dagger
of truth, or let her live in hope, and add another
flower of deceit to her garden of self-deception?

The truth is a killer and a thief.

Tear down the walls of all our homes, drop the
make-believe that makes life worth living, release
all the drapes of wish and courtesy and considera-

tion and noble conduct and what have you? Biological facts infested with selfish desires.

It is the make-believe and the will to believe that make the world a livable place.

Truly, aren't the poets liars? Or does she really walk like a dream?

Aren't the musicians liars? Surely, there are no sounds in the forest or on the street or at the ocean or in the cave that are like the music fairy tales of Mozart or Bach or Beethoven.

Aren't the painters liars? The meadow is never that green (a real meadow is a rocky, weedy field dotted by patches of manure).

Aren't sculptors liars, or have you really seen a face like Michaelangelo's Moses?

Aren't philosophers liars? They don't really hunt for the truth. The truth is easily found, but it's simple and it's boring and it's petty. They hunt for the lie, for the most magnificent lie, the lie that carries them away, out of this realm of everyday things.

Aren't the prophets liars? Why should God speak to them and not to you, and speak with aeonic vehemence so you may never doubt Him?

Perhaps the tales of the prophets will bring to your ears the divine utterances of the Holy Spirit.

Aren't the statesmen liars, and the revolutionaries who fantasy those ever attractive Utopias, where men would behave not as they really do, but as Homeric beings?

All these lies of the poets, the artists, the prophets—they make us better, they make us finer and kinder and hopeful and good.

The lie is the road to perfection; the truth is but an obstacle.

YOUR LOVING

FATHER

Wisdom of the Body

MY DEAR SON,

The mind needs cultivating, just as does the body. Without cultivation it deteriorates. The mind needs proper nourishment just like the body —a diversified diet containing the basic spiritual elements.

And the mind needs exercise and relaxation. If this care is not given it, sooner or later the mind betrays this neglect by becoming shallow and confused.

A thousand substances go into the nourishment of the human body. And there are some the body can not do without. A thousand ideas go into the nourishment of the human soul, and there are some the soul is unable to do without. It can be said that three-fourths of mankind is physically undernourished. Of much more than three-fourths of mankind can it be said that it is emotionally and intellectually grossly underfed.

The progress of mankind has been made on only a fraction of its intellect. Even today, the potential intellectual power of millions of men remains undeveloped because of inferior economic conditions and lack of schooling.

The fine arts, the drama, poetry and prose from the pens of writers of true calling, and last, but not least, the writings of those concerned with the problems of our inner life—these are the basic foods the mind cannot do without. Denied these stimuli, the mind of man withers, like a plant deprived of water and minerals. We have a fancy name for men with such dried up minds; we call them "extroverts," because they have lost all introversion and introspection. They are just shells of humans, moving through life mechanically, responding automatically to the requirements of modern society. They live a stereotyped life in the patterns impressed upon them by the matrix of school, family, and business. In them there is no inner motivation or consciousness of issues or problems other than those of their own dull, daily routine.

There is a kind of wisdom in the body, too, that mysterious functioning responsible for so many of our actions before reasoning and speculation take place. Those little deeds of infants and small children that cause amazement in their parents are born of the wisdom of the body. And many of the actions and attitudes of adults are the result, not of thought, but of sheer body wisdom.

Fear, wonder, cheer, faith—there is great spiritual and mental power hidden in the body. They are the products of a complex structure as intricate as the mechanico-physical organization responsible for functions such as digestion, blood circulation, and glandular action. They operate without our direction or awareness, unless their normal function is disturbed.

YOUR LOVING

FATHER

Treat Gently the Abnormal

My dear Son,

The philosopher Kant once said that truth and normalcy are equivalent to what is generally accepted as being so. If this were the case, then the norm for this world would depend upon the mentality and artistry of a Chinese coolie, or an Indian rice-farmer, or an American liquor salesman; for, in number at least, those come as close to generality as Kant could have wished.

However, all the achievements of this world have been made by abnormal people. The unrelenting efforts of the genius, who frequently drives himself to the detriment of his health, wealth and social position, are certainly not symptomatic of normalcy. History is full of examples of the weaknesses, diseases and even decadence of the great: Beethoven, Schubert, Hoelderlin, Shelley, Dostoiewsky, Poe, Schopenhauer, Lenin, Lenau, Nietzsche, Wilde. Perhaps some day we will discover what links disease with genius.

Chinese physicians once argued that great singers probably possess very sick throats because a normal throat could not sing as sweetly and as loudly. Edison thought inventors ought to cultivate one-track minds, and one-track minds are not normal.

And the religious leaders of centuries gone by, or even the Latter-Day-Saints, can anyone claim they were normal? Mohammed heard voices in the desert and conversed with the angel Gabriel as I talk to you now. Moses heard voices from the burning bush; Jesus related messages from the Lord; and Joseph Smith beheld a vision of golden plates containing the Mormon Gospel. Were these persons normal? Still the world bows before their wisdom and admits their visions to faith. Saint Francis of Assisi could hear the birds speak; Daniel could speak to the lions; Eckehard was certain there was a tiny flame burning in his chest; Holy Theresa could feel in her hands and legs the wounds that the Roman soldiers inflicted upon Christ, in fact, she could show the blood upon them; Luther could see the very devil on the wall and throw his inkwell at him. Can we call these people normal?

Plato called poetry a kind of mania. Lombroso wrote a large volume on genius and insanity. A contemporary physician compiled a comprehensive manuscript on music and disease.

The world of accomplishments is full of one-sidedness, of idiosyncrasy, peculiarity and mysterious defects. Perhaps some day we will find the key to the dark background of the fantastic world of genius.

Until then: Treat gently the abnormal, he may carry some subtle talent under the cloud of his peculiarities.

YOUR LOVING

FATHER

The Quest for Happiness

My dear Son,

The quest for happiness, in its intensity, is second only to the search for bread. When man began to contemplate the meaning of his being, he began his search for happiness.

If happiness is the enjoyment of the present, perennial happiness means continuous enjoyment. How arduous, then, must be the task of finding a formula for a truly gratifying way of life.

In all matters germane to philosophy, our knowledge is limited to the written thoughts of men. Yet it is possible that some of the deepest theorems were devised by men of silence who never publicized the ideas they lived by. Some of the most vital thinkers were rather loath to preach, and others were reluctant to write: Laotse, Herakleitos, Socrates, Baal-Shem Tov.

The earliest documents relating to the philosophical quest for happiness are to be found in the literature of the ancient Hebrews, especially in the books attributed to Solomon, King of the Hebrews. We find in these writings many theorems of human conduct which grew out of the pondering of the ancient Israelites.

From these roots flowered the great literature of the Orient and the Occident. The beginnings of moral philosophy, east and west of the Jordan, can be traced to the small nation living on that river in the year 1000 B.C. or earlier. This is not so strange when we consider that some very simple minds have true philosophic wit and wisdom. For it comes with the desire to know more than appears on the surface. And one can be a great scientist and still be a poor philosopher.

All your life you will search for lasting enjoyment of the present. Is such lasting enjoyment possible? And if it is, what mastery of the mind or body is necessary to achieve such a state?

And who are the happy? Are they the poor in mind? Are they those who are drawn into themselves, hermit-like? Are they the faithful, never disturbed in their belief? Are they the connoisseurs of life's hedonistic pleasures? Are they the men of stoic resignation, never troubled by the storms of life? Are they the meditators? Are they the scientists trained in self-discipline?

Are they the careless? The ambitious? The indifferent? The sensuous? The dreamers? The cogitators? The domineering or the dominated? The submissive? The escapists?

Wherein lies the unfailing answer to this perennial quest?

Of this I am certain: No answer can be given, the answer must be found.

YOUR LOVING

FATHER

Love and Desire

My dear Son,

You have asked me how one knows he is in love. True love creates a feeling of pleasure, born of the act of giving. Love that takes is desire, with true love being a sensation of happiness accompanied by giving. The true lover wants all the world to love his chosen one and he is constantly proselytizing among friends and strangers for the glory of his beloved.

It is this exuberance that is the basis of poetry and the other creative arts, that makes one wish to create, to poetize, to pen and sing and sculpt, and praise the beauty of the loved one.

Plato once called this love a kind of ecstasy. Spinoza identified it as having the same origin as our love for the creative Universe.

Of course, even such love has its jealousy; fear that the idol may become lost in the drabness and evil of an everyday world. It is fear, not desire, that creates such jealousy; the fear of losing the pearl in the gravel. There is no love without jealousy. True love has its jealousy even as lust and possessive desire; but jealousies are as different as the motives that inspire them.

YOUR LOVING

FATHER

Books to Live By

MY DEAR SON,

I wish there were a copyright from God that would prevent those patchwork efforts of fleeting shrewdness and fancy from being called books. For a book is a holy thing; a *real* book is.

In ancient Israel when one spoke of the Book, he meant the Book of Law, the Book of Wisdom, the Book of Proverbs.

Indeed, the Greek word for book is *biblion*—the Bible. There was a time in our country, not much more than a hundred years ago, when the average man exclaimed: "The Book says . . . !"—meaning the Bible. A special place in the house was reserved for the Book, and I am not speaking metaphorically.

Today the Bible means little in our country, or in any other country, for that matter. When people speak of "The Book" today, they probably mean *Forever Amber.*

I suppose you can still find the Bible in every home—Christian or whatever they call it; you will have to look for it in the attic though, or on the bottom shelf of the bookcase, by the side of outdated catalogues and atlases. Yes, even the hotels keep a Bible on the night-table, for the tired salesman and other travelers trying to sober up. It is a clever move of the Bible societies, but you cannot resurrect Christianity with publicity schemes. Bibles are still being published by the million, but the fire which illuminated the books cannot kindle the ice in the hearts of the callous Christians of our time.

Show me the books in your house and I will tell you what you are. Show me the books by which you live.

Perhaps there are no books at all in your house, only the books that come with the dirt and go with the wind.

You may never find a friend but you can always find a book. And with books as your friends, you will not go through life a lonely man.

YOUR LOVING

FATHER

Life of the Common Man

My dear Son,

The average history book youth is blessed with studying is largely a chronicle of the continuous warfare among the Western nations, with a few scant remarks on peace-time activities squeezed in between martial descriptions.

True historiography should tell of the peaceful activities of man with perhaps some occasional references showing how warfare disturbed them.

The kind of Caesarian history now written permits the teen-age scholar to acquire considerable information regarding the armor and military campaigns of sixteenth century Germany, France, or England, without having the slightest knowledge of the life, science and social conditions in those countries. This same much abused scholar, shackled to the silly textbooks by the chain of an antiquated system of pedagogy, might know all the princes and rulers of the last thirty centuries, but little would he be aware of how, where and when the standards of life of the common man were raised and by whom and why and how?

He may know a lot about Alexander and Caesar and Attila and Ghengis Khan and Napoleon, and King Frederick, but ask him about the men who did the great and lasting jobs in scientific and social revolution, and how bitter their struggles were, and how the people lived or existed during all the centuries of bombastic conquerors! Ask him, and you will discover how much he needs to know of true history, the story of man's conquest over the evil in man and the vicissitudes of nature.

YOUR LOVING

FATHER

Is He the Savior?

My dear Son,

The pernicious theology of the crucifixion, which makes a great issue of the alleged execution by the Romans of a man who claimed to be the Messiah, has cost the lives of millions of other Jews, Jews like Jesus himself. In fact, all the important figures around Jesus were Jews—such as the rabbinical student Saul, known as St. Paul; the fisherman Shimon, known as St. Peter, the fisherman Levi, known as St. Matthew, and the others.

Jesus regarded himself as a Jew, thoroughly Mosaic. As he stated, "I did not come to destroy the Torah, but to fulfill it." He ate matzos at the time of Passover. He obeyed all the ritual laws. He observed the laws of clothing. Indeed, if you wish to know what Jesus looked like, you will not find his likeness *Unter Den Linden,* or in the streets of Dublin; look for it in the ghettos of New York or London. There you may also find the descendants of the children of Mary, those who have not been gassed or hung by the Christian Germans.

The theology of crucifixion is dangerous because it stamps the Jews as the destroyers of religion, and makes of the whole disbelieving Western world just one beautiful herd of the faithful. Historically, the opposite is correct. The Jews established the belief in the one and only God, whose will, wish and very nature are justice. Jews, too, have created the Christian religion, with its academic "Love thy neighbor as thyself." I say academic because, historically speaking, all that the Christians and their neighbors have done for the past two thousand years is persecute the Jews and destroy them. In the name of this fantastic love religion—which is as unnatural to man as hate comes easy to the Western world—this fantastic love religion has placed on its altar in the very face of the cross the blood of six million Jews without batting a hypocritical eyelash. Not a single believing Christian German, of the seventy million, stood up and said, "Nay, let us not murder." Not a single German Christian preacher or priest has come forth—after all the gory details of

the German pogrom orgy have been made known
—and asked for anything but sympathy for his
poor accused fellow German Christians.

Hidden deep in this gigantic religious mockery
lies the reason for the Hebrew rejection of Jesus
as the Messiah. The whole fantastic theology of
crucifixion notwithstanding, the Jews doubted and
rejected the Platonic love theories of Jesus because man can be made to follow the precepts of
Divine Justice, but man never will (he never has)
really accept the so-called "Love thy neighbor
as thyself" theorem of the New Testament. It always was, and still is, a sham and a chimera, the
hypocrisy and pretense behind which has always
operated the thoroughly selfish and brutal disbelieving Western world.

Who burned alive and gassed and tortured six
million Jewish men, women and children? The
great German Christian nation. Who stoned to
death forty-one Jews in front of a Church? The
Christian Polish citizens of Kielce. And of the
many thousands of Christian priests in Poland,
only one, one single one, came out openly to con-
demn such pogroms.

The Hungarian Christians and the Romanian

Christians, the Spanish Christians and the Austrian Christians, and the murders and wars and persecutions and burnings and hangings by the Europeans of colonial people all over the globe, the suppression of the poor by the wealthy, the keeping of slaves by Christian property owners . . . Where shall I begin? Where shall I end? How can I possibly enumerate all the gigantic bestialities perpetrated during the last two thousand years by adherents to the Christian faith? Remember, this is the faith based upon the creed: "Love thy neighbor." The Jews never trusted that creed. They stood fast and held to their faith in the one God and the prophetic truth of justice. How different a world would this be, if justice had prevailed over love—this sickening hypocrisy of Christian love, with blood on its hands and a lie in its throat.

What blasphemy is this theology of crucifixion —to paint the Jew as the destroyer of religion when the Jew is really its creator! The theology of crucifixion is the perennial incitement to Jew-hating and pogromism.

YOUR LOVING

FATHER

The Ungrateful Hand

My dear Son,

The Jew has given our Western world the one true God, the great Book of Wisdom and Poetry, whence our literature and art sprang;—even the instruments of our music: Harp, flute, drum, trumpet, cymbal, came to us through the Jew.

What have the people of the Western world given the Jew? They burned the Jewish temple, made torches of Jewish bodies, and bonfires of Jewish books.

Perhaps the people of the Western world hate the Jew because he gave them so much. The Chinese, Indians, and Japanese never hated the Jew; they never got anything from him. The hate carriers of the Jew took even their theology from the Jew: The God who became man and claimed to be a son of David, and the faithful band of Jewish fishermen and shepherds who believed in the claims of the new Messiah.

The Jews brought the Holy Fire to the West;
the West wrung it from their hands and threw its
bearers into the pit.

What would the world, our Western world, be
without the Jews? Remove the traces of Jewish
steps and the world would go back five thousand
years.

Look out of your window, and what do you
see? The spire of the church built for the son of
Miriam, a silent, tender Jewess. Step into your
museums, take from the walls the paintings which
have a Jewish theme, and you remove the most
glorious works of Rembrandt, Rafael Santi, Leonardo, Michaelangelo, and many of the other
masters.

Go to your bookshelf and pull out the books
that carry reference to Jews. You will have to
eliminate the books of Christian and Moslem theology, the great works of Shakespeare, the works
of Milton, Dante and Herder, of Byron, Chaucer
and Goethe.

There is no man or woman in art or literature
who did not draw strength and inspiration from
the Holy Fire of the Jewish soul.

And how they did try to squelch this ever-burning flame!

YOUR LOVING

FATHER

Teachers and Tumblers

My dear Son,

Education is rarely the basis of human reasoning. In matters of opinion, including the opinionated sciences such as history, anthropology, philosophy and law, people are driven by their emotions toward a desired conclusion; the so-called mind merely supplies the necessary rationalization.

These differences in conclusion are not due to differences in our thinking processes but to dissimilar emotional, frequently even opportunistic, attitudes.

A man like Aristotle, a servant of his King, could look upon the Sophists, who pleaded for man's equality before God, as tricksters desiring to upset the "god-created" equilibrium of Slave-nations on the one hand and Free-born (of course, his own) people on the other.

The thinking of people usually depends upon which side their bread is buttered. This is especially true of the thinking done by the teaching profession in countries where the state administration does all the buttering.

As a rule, teachers are some of the least free of men in their written expression. A little paper-hanger was able to seize control of a great state and hundreds of thousands of teachers from primary schools to universities jumped on the wagon to prove that the paper-hanger's cockeyed emotional outbursts had a deep scientific basis. Reason frequently seems to be a very obedient servant of emotion and opportunistic desires. There is a library crammed with books on history, philosophy, literature, anthropology, law, economics and sociology to prove by reason what one ignorant tyrant considered reasonable. But these obvious examples of German reason since King Frederick the Great are not the only ones. All opinionated knowledge in the era of Christian dominance was deeply colored by the cross or the sword.

In everyday life it is prejudice which determines people's judgment; prejudice nourished through the formative years by a onesided and narrow education.

It is in the furrow of hate and love, profit and loss, advantage and disadvantage, that the poor little flower of reason grows.

There is no other way of reasoning. The only question is: Does your reason thrive on love or hate, on advantage to all or your mean little self?

YOUR LOVING
FATHER

Presumptuous Artist

My dear Son,

Have you ever come across the bully-artist?

There are limitations to the significance and the merits of the arts and the artist. Perhaps minor presumptions can be forgiven the artist, even an overbearing temperament, sincere or assumed. But the realm of art is not so poor as to have to tolerate downright viciousness and cussedness. The world can do without the works of Richard Wagner, Richard Strauss, and their like. We can more easily do without their music than put up with the venom they carried in their lives and actions.

There is no absolute art, but there is absolute evil. Let us throw away the Grail filled with the wine of Lucifer, and let us cast away the treacherous rapier of the Rosenkavalier, even if that will break the cup and the sword.

YOUR LOVING
FATHER

Hear, O Israel

My dear Son,

The only true and perfect definition of Deity is the Hebrew *Shmah Israel Adonai Elohainou Adonai Echod.* [Hear, O Israel, the Lord is God; the Lord is One.]

This majestic exclamation of the Torah is the one and true word of God. It is *Logos* and *idea.* In God you can find yourself. Your innermost self leads to Him. In your innermost self you will find Him. *Tatwam-atsi:* Whatever you see is Yourself.

After the great *Shmah Israel* had struck the hearts of the chosen sons of the desert many sermons were spoken and many books on theology were written. A stream of words came forth from the mouths of the exhilarated, the inspired, the fearful, the hopeful—but these were just words. Deep words, to be sure, uttered by prophetic lips, and also small tales, fables, and legends told and

retold by timid and sometimes paganly superstitious frightened faithful.

Shmah Israel Adonai Elohainou Adonai Echod
is the all of monistic theology. The substance is
revealed by its very definition. This is God's own
theology. All else is the word of man, and how
varied and contradictory it is. We know only from
hearsay that such words were ever spoken.

How many of these words are interpolated?
How much is truth, and how much falsehood?
What does it matter, if only we have grasped and
been grasped by the thunderous *Shmah Israel?*

YOUR LOVING
FATHER

Sanctified Devils

My dear Son,

A biography, as written by a third person, describes only the shell of its subject. The true being of man will always remain a mystery, even to the closest of observers. Men may be villains and act as saints; men may be saints and appear to their neighbors as the incarnation of deviltry.

How many saints were burned at the stake? And how many devils were sanctified?

The world and history judge a man by what he does, or appears to do, or by what he neglects to do. Always this curtain of appearance hides man's true essence, his motives, his desires and his inner life.

YOUR LOVING
FATHER

Ancient Ancestors

MY DEAR SON,

History in its various applications concerns it-self with little more than five thousand years. We split the millions of years of existing mankind into a hundred different groups, races, and types, al-though our concrete knowledge of their past and their background covers only five thousand years.

What do all these national and racial separa-tions mean, if we, for only a moment, push aside the word-cloud of pseudo-history and pseudo-ethnology and steal a glimpse into our far, far-away past? Perhaps somewhere on a treeless mountaintop, we can spy a herd of early humans, cowering close to a cave, in fear of the elements and beasts.

How little do we know of man's past and how much do we make of that little we know.

YOUR LOVING

FATHER

Bloody Sickle

My dear Son,

Communism—what a majestic thought: That those who have nothing to lose—the proletarians—unite in a commune of socialistic endeavor. Ah, for the grandiose dreams that have enlivened the hopes of nations and poets. Some of those dreams grew to reality among the Incas, others in the unhappy experiments of Plato, and some among the religious sects of 19th century America.

What grandiose dreams, only to vanish at the destroying touch of man's colossal callousness and egotism. The proletarians unite, but it is a shallow and hollow unity under the aegis of shrewd, self-seeking politicians, and gone from the bloody hammer and sickle is the glimmer of Marxist love of man for man, and freedom for all.

YOUR LOVING
FATHER

Crime and Punishment

My dear Son,

Our jails are schools in perversion. Cunningly organized by dungeon minds, these institutions harden offenders and make criminals of the erring. One of their diabolical schemes is the separation of individuals from their families. Certainly, crimes against society should be punished, but why punish society by perverting the offender and his family?

How does society expect to correct the character and attitude of an offender, if he is subjected to the cage life of an animal? They too have half an hour's time a day to roam in the open yard.

The biologically normal man must become perverted in mind, body, and soul by this form of medieval seclusion; not to speak of the biological and emotional confusion created in the offender's wife or husband by the year-long separation.

Perhaps the Soviets have found a solution in the creation of isolated labor camps where offenders may lead a normal family and social life. Such a form of punishment is severe enough for most of what is labeled "crime" in our society, and such punishment doesn't create, as do our penal institutions, the great army of punks, pimps, fairies and bums. You cannot make a man straight by having him live a crooked jail-life. There is nothing normal in jail-life as we enforce it—neither living nor sleeping nor working nor eating, not even the clothing. Men and women can be punished for most of their offenses without robbing them of their dignity, humanity, and that sense of social responsibility that may lead them back to a normal life. Men separated from their mates for three, five and ten years will never be normal again. Why must escape-proof prisons force their inmates to wear silly stripes and keep them preoccupied with moronic tasks?

Why not open, throughout the country, penal villages where offenders may live with their families and serve their time in a normal way, living and working a straight life, from whence they would return, still punished, but better?

YOUR LOVING

FATHER

Cannibals and Pets

MY DEAR SON,

Some day, many, many years hence, we will be
charged with cannibalism for cutting the throats
of animal beings so similar to ourselves, and de-
vouring them. The flesh and bone structure of
these animals is so much like our own, and even
their taste so similar, that it has happened that
fiends served "long pig" (that is what some abori-
gines call human flesh) instead of animal meat.

It is amazing to see how much fuss some people
make over certain types of animals, like dogs, cats
and horses. They pet them, wash them, take them
to bed, become despondent when they get lost,
even talk to them and caress them. On the other
hand, the very same people may take animals
raised in the same way, such as cows, deer, or
goats, and without any particular ado, string them
up, cut their throats, and devour them—half raw,
cooked, or just chopped. In fact, the animals kept

by one people as friends and pets, even objects of veneration, may be found, with another people, in the daily meat pot.

Basically, the elevation of common animals to the alleged status of friendship, devotion, or even veneration, is as silly as the butchering of the same animals by others is distasteful.

Man should have no difficulty in replacing the traditional barbaric flesh foods with plant and synthetic nourishment. And if man yearns for comradeship or desires to exercise his protective instincts, he would do much better to adopt a human friend or one of the millions of Asia's and Europe's orphans, instead of taking to himself a gutter-licking dog or a malodorous cat. The world is poor enough in kindness and affection. Why waste it on animals? Humans need it, and need it badly.

Animal protection is rather an affectation in a world that does not protect its humans.

YOUR LOVING
FATHER

Evening Thoughts

MY DEAR SON,

Age is not determined by the years a man has lived, but rather by those he will live. Man's true age lies in the life span ahead of him, not the span behind him.

In no two people does maturity occur at the same time. Some mature at the age of ten, as do prodigies in music; some, like poets, at the age of twenty. These persons frequently drop into obscurity after their early accomplishments. Some mature in the evening of their lives, like Leonardo and Voltaire, soaring suddenly after an uneventful life.

* * *

Beware of envy. A man with mouse eyes can see little but the heels of another man.

* * *

Loneliness is not an attribute only of the very

great. The very dull, too, can be lonely. The great can be alone because they enjoy companionship with their rich inner-self. The very dull are alone because they lack the initiative to absorb what comes their way.

*   *   *

Live as you think, and live thoughtfully.

*   *   *

Some of history's most important men went into oblivion within their lifetime. They held no official positions and left little or nothing on clay or parchment.

How frequently in history the burden rests on men behind the screen; the fancy and proud actors on the stage were only marionettes.

*   *   *

If you are not willing to deny someone's authority, you have no right to accept it. You have just as little right to say "Yes" to something you do not understand, as you have to say "No."

Servility is a form of inverted arrogance.

You cannot train a horse with shouts and expect it to obey a whisper.

*　　*　　*

There are many hidden energies in the universe. We probably see them at work every day and still do not know them;—as mankind saw the workings of electricity for a million years without being aware of its nature.

*　　*　　*

Intuition is thinking ahead, as reason is thinking back. Just as we have memory for things that have occurred in the past, there may be in our minds, in conformity with the physical and spiritual unity of the universe, an instinctive knowledge of what is to occur. Intuition is the pure and otherwise unexplainable form of cognition of events in being.

*　　*　　*

Abstention is a way of life, and so is indulgence. In themselves they are neither good nor bad. They only become good or bad so far as they affect society. It is what we do to others, or fail to

do for others, that matters. What we do with ourselves is no one's business but our own. I wonder
if even God cares. Only Nature has a right to punish the self-indulgence in man, and Nature does.

* * *

YOUR LOVING
FATHER